This Walker book
belongs to:

rithee good folk, listen to me!

Her most noble Majesty Queen Elizabeth I, who recently departed this world, had no children. Thus she was the last of our great Tudor monarchs. Before Her Majesty died, she bid me write down tales from Tudor times for your pleasure, both tragical and comical.

I was in my tenth year when I came to Queen Elizabeth's court, and I soon became her favourite scribe. I hope that I have done Her Majesty justice in writing these tales, and that they will help me leave my mark on the realm. So, I entreat you, read on. I will try to entertain you right royally!

Arthur Inkblott
May 1603

PS — Beneath the Tudor tales you will find scenes from the lives of Tudor common folk. At the last count there were some four million of these peasants in all of England and Wales.

PPS — Pray allow me to introduce my ferret, Smudge. He lives in the margins of this book and has much to say. Yet, I beseech you, be careful, for he has often nipped a passing finger!

For
Thom,
with
love.

Off with his head!

Just a joke!

First published 2015 by Walker Books Ltd
87 Vauxhall Walk, London SE11 5HJ
This edition published 2016
2 4 6 8 10 9 7 5 3 1

Text and illustrations © 2015 Marcia Williams

The right of Marcia Williams to be identified as author/illustrator of this work has been
asserted by her in accordance with the Copyright, Designs and Patents Act 1988

This book has been typeset in Truesdell, Yuletide and Perry Gothic
Printed in China

British Library Cataloguing in Publication Data:
a catalogue record for this book is available from the British Library

ISBN 978-1-4063-6581-8

THE TUDORS

Kings · Queens · Scribes · and · Ferrets ·

WRITTEN AND ILLUSTRATED BY

MARCIA WILLIAMS

HELPED BY ARTHUR INKBLOTT

WALKER BOOKS

AND SUBSIDIARIES

LONDON · BOSTON · SYDNEY · AUCKLAND

The Wars of the Roses

For 30 years, a great civil war raged across England. I was not alive to witness it, but it is still spoken of with awe. It was caused by two noble families, known as houses, fighting for the right to rule. One was the House of York, whose symbol was a white rose, and the other the House of Lancaster, whose symbol was a red rose, so the battles were known as the Wars of the Roses. I tremble to imagine how long these wars might have raged if Henry Tudor, a noble Welshman from the House of Lancaster, had not arrived in England.

· MOST PEOPLE LIVED IN THE COUNTRY OR IN SMALL MARKET TOWNS

The Battle of Bosworth Field

Henry Tudor led his troops against the unpopular King Richard III, of the House of York. They met at Bosworth Field in Leicestershire where they fought the last great battle of the Wars of the Roses on 22 August 1485. Although King Richard bravely defended his crown, many of his soldiers and their noble commanders defected to Henry's side – and so King Richard was slain! His crown fell from his helmet and rolled beneath a bush. From there it was retrieved and placed on Henry's head, and the reign of the Tudors began – or so the minstrels sing!

• LIFE WAS NOT EASY • JOBS WERE FEW AND MANY STRUGGLED TO SCRAPE A LIVING •

Who Was Henry Tudor?

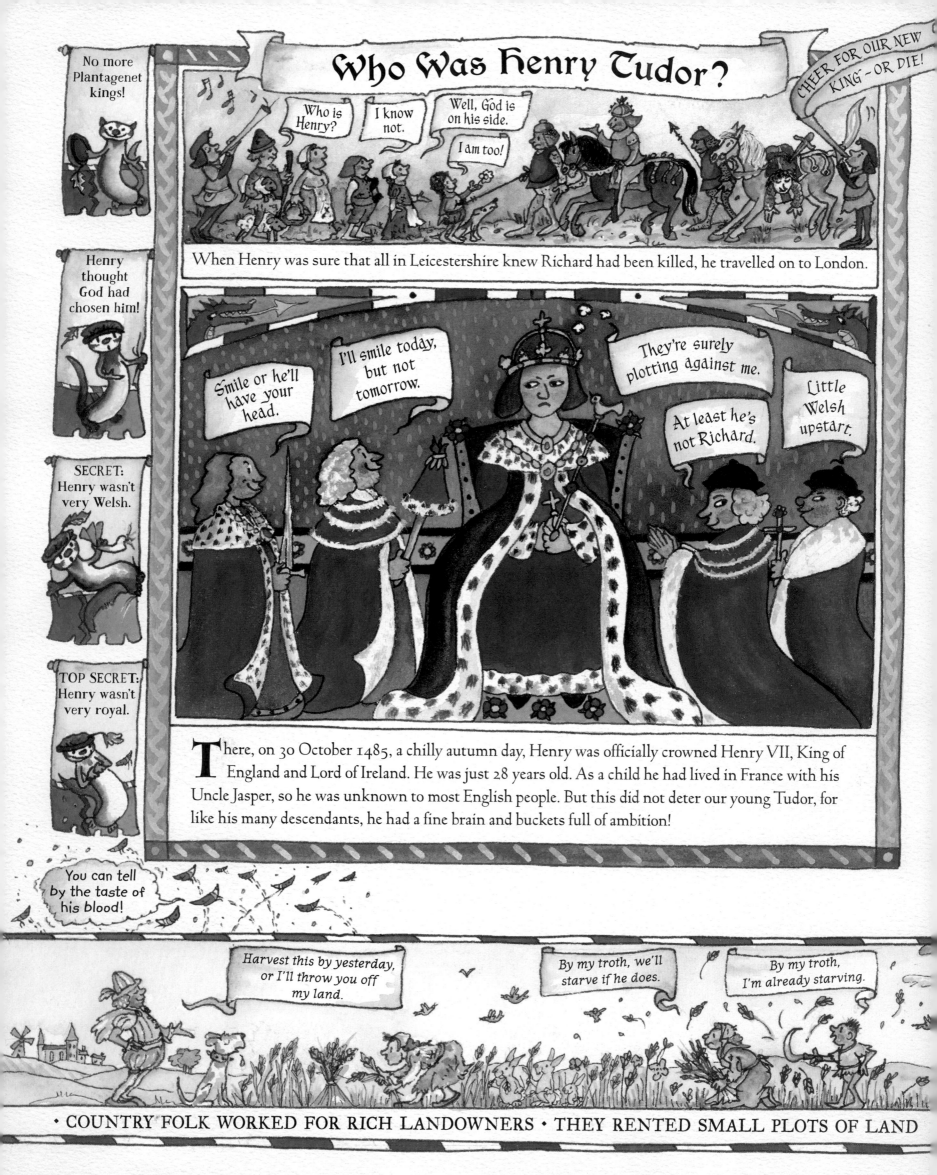

When Henry was sure that all in Leicestershire knew Richard had been killed, he travelled on to London.

There, on 30 October 1485, a chilly autumn day, Henry was officially crowned Henry VII, King of England and Lord of Ireland. He was just 28 years old. As a child he had lived in France with his Uncle Jasper, so he was unknown to most English people. But this did not deter our young Tudor, for like his many descendants, he had a fine brain and buckets full of ambition!

• COUNTRY FOLK WORKED FOR RICH LANDOWNERS • THEY RENTED SMALL PLOTS OF LAND

Henry was born at Pembroke Castle, Wales, in January 1457.

His father, Edmund Tudor, died before his birth.

His mother, Margaret Beaufort, was thirteen when he was born!

Most girls married aged fourteen.

Henry's father had no claim to the throne.

Henry's mother could trace her ancestry back to Edward III.

YOU WILL NEVER BE SAFE FROM US, HENRY VII!

At least twelve people had more right to the throne than Henry.

Ferrets marry from eight months!

Including his poor young mother!

This made Henry feel very insecure.

He had won the crown, but how would he keep it?

Traitors risked torture ...

or even execution!

Torture sours the blood.

TO GROW THEIR OWN CROPS AND GRAZED THEIR FEW ANIMALS ON COMMON LAND ·

Henry VII Rewrites History!

Henry won the Battle of Bosworth Field, so Parliament believed God had chosen him as king. But a goodly number of nobles thought he had no right to the throne. Henry had to act fast to stop them raising armies against him, so he declared that his reign had started the day *before* the battle. This meant everyone who had supported Richard III was a traitor – and Henry executed many of them, chip, chop, aaagh! He threw the rest into the Tower of London. If they tried to escape, he executed them too!

A Royal Wedding

Hurrah for King Henry VII!

This will bring peace.

Verily, she is most fair.

Hurrah for them both!

If Henry was to hold on to his crown, he needed to do more than execute a few unfriendly nobles. So he married Elizabeth of York, even though he had never met her before the wedding, to unite his House of Lancaster with her House of York. On the day of the wedding, London was thronged with cheering crowds. Everyone hoped that the marriage would bring peace to England.

Henry cleverly joined his red rose of Lancaster with the white rose of York to create the Tudor Rose. He plastered his new rose everywhere he could think of, including buildings, coins, flags and banners. Now even his most illiterate subjects would see that it was their great Tudor monarch, Henry VII, who had united the houses and brought an end to the War of the Roses!

A great way of defeating the Yorkists!

Tudor monarchs had great brains ...

but did they have great morals?

Zzzzzzzzzz...

He'll DEFINITELY lozzze his head!

No lice today.

Money

Henry never imposed a ferret tax.

Maybe he didn't fancy being the first fingerless king!

Tudor monarchs liked absolute power.

Henry liked getting his own way!

I will banish you if you keep fighting!

Henry VII won his crown in battle, but he was no warrior.

Is there not even one groat?

Not one, sire.

Wars were expensive and Henry had inherited a very poor realm.

No new gowns, no wine, cheap beer...

To save money he cut palace spending, including the queen's.

Poor nobles are more loyal.

PRITHEE, PAY YOUR TAXES HERE

PAY UP OR DIE!

I can't afford a sword, let alone an uprising.

Then, to refill England's empty purses, he imposed heavy taxes – especially on wealthy nobles. This increased the country's wealth, but it did not help Henry's popularity.

Pay £10,000 to guarantee your loyalty and I'll say no more about the poisoned wine.

Henry also created a system of bonds so that displeasing him became very costly.

Guilty! A large fine or death?

I'll take the fine.

He set up the Star Chamber, a court where even the most powerful lords could be tried and fined!

Henry's full title: Henry, by the Grace of God, King of England, France and Lord of Ireland.

I'm flipping exhausted!

Stop moaning woman, I've been up since cockcrow.

We all work hard.

Spare us some beer.

That I will, friend.

· PEASANT WOMEN WORKED VERY HARD · THEY CLEANED AND COOKED AND LOOKED

Power

I hope those uniforms are second-hand!

Henry used some of his newly acquired wealth to increase his own security. He was the first English monarch to have his own bodyguards: the Yeomen of the Guard.

I'm the only power here.

I see that now!

Henry made it illegal for nobles to raise private armies.

Keep your ears and eyes open!

He also created a network of spies across England and Europe.

Not a bad week's haul.

Anyone reported to be plotting against him was executed.

Order of the Garter! Sounds good ~ costs nothing!

He did reward loyal subjects, but only if it didn't cost too much!

I even worry in my sleep!

Henry ruled for nearly 24 years, but he was never able to stop worrying about money or plots to steal his crown!

Henry liked large presents.

Lots of large presents ...

land, money or castles!

Fleas prefer a dog to a human.

Depends which is juiciest!

Stop nursing 'im, he'll only die.

I 'ates churning butter.

But I loves eating it.

Baa!

Ye'll be mutton stew if ye don't give us more wool!

AFTER THE CHILDREN • THEY MADE BUTTER, CHEESE, BEER AND THE FAMILY CLOTHES •

Christopher Columbus

COLUMBUS' FIRST VOYAGE

NORTH AMERICA

ENGLAND

ATLANTIC OCEAN

SPAIN

Early Tudor maps weren't accurate.

America wasn't on them.

Columbus navigated by the sun and the stars.

Only two of his three ships made it home.

Land ahoy!

During Henry VII's reign, most learned men thought that the world was flat, and that ships would fall off the edge if they sailed too far. But Italian navigator Christopher Columbus believed the world was round. He decided to sail west to find a new, safer route to Asia, which was rich in treasure. In 1492, supported by Queen Isabella of Spain, Columbus set off. After many weeks he sighted land. Columbus thought he had reached East Asia, and he returned to Spain a hero! He died never knowing that he hadn't found a shortcut to Asia ... he had discovered America!

In fourteen hundred and ninety-two, Columbus sailed the ocean blue.

Go yonder and call the midwife.

I go!

I go too, for this is women's work.

18 HOURS LATER

Lord, 'tis but a puny thing.

· WOMEN OFTEN DIED IN CHILDBIRTH OR FROM AN INFECTION AFTER THE BABY WAS BORN ·

Columbus had asked Henry VII to fund the voyage, but Henry thought it too risky; he was more interested in the arts and new ideas coming from Europe than in exploration. He encouraged French and Italian scholars and artists to visit England. He also supported England's first printer, William Caxton, causing many scribes to fear for their jobs! But when Henry heard that Columbus had returned with exotic treasures including turkeys, parrots and gold, he changed his mind about sea voyages! So in 1497 he sent his own explorer, John Cabot, off to seek treasure in North America.

• A WOMAN'S AVERAGE LIFE EXPECTANCY WAS ONLY 35 YEARS •

Henry VII's Family

A son was vital to a king.

A spare son was an extra bonus.

Girls didn't usually inherit the crown.

Women were born to serve and obey!

Arthur Tudor

Margaret Tudor

Henry, Duke of York

Mary Tudor

Henry VII had married Elizabeth to save his crown, but she was kind and clever and he grew to love her. They had eight children, although only four survived infancy.

"A" is for apple.

Elizabeth taught her children to read and write.

"T" is for Tudors.

Henry helped the tutors teach his sons history.

I am the best!

He made sure they had the best tutors available.

That's my boy — we are the greats!

Henry favoured his eldest son, Arthur, heir to the crown and his hope for a Tudor dynasty!

All the more time to enjoy my sports!

His youngest son, Henry, was just a spare. He was not expected to take on royal duties.

The king was in his counting house, counting out his money. The queen was in the parlour, eating bread and honey.

One night's wee!

That's nothing, watch this!

Poo!

I was going to drink that!

• OPEN SEWERS RAN THROUGH THE STREETS AND SEWAGE CONTAMINATED RIVERS •

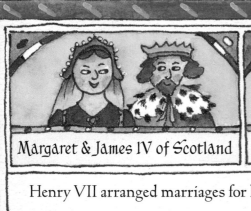

Margaret & James IV of Scotland

Mary & Louis XII of France

Arthur & Catherine of Aragon

Henry VII arranged marriages for his children to help keep the peace with neighbouring countries.

I may not be so spare after all!

In 1502, six months after marrying, Arthur died of a fever.

We will have another child.

Henry VII was devastated, but he was comforted by Elizabeth.

You're all I have left.

In 1503, Elizabeth gave birth to a daughter. She and the baby died.

Can't I go outside?

No. Help me make money!

Henry retired to his privy chamber at Richmond Palace to mourn. He stayed there for most of his final years. Henry VII had avoided foreign conflict and brought peace and prosperity to England – not bad for an unknown Welshman. The Tudor monarchy was off to a strong start and Arthur's younger brother Henry was ready and waiting to carry on the Tudor dynasty!

Ferrets get to choose their mates!

Infant death was very common.

Henry never married again.

The fleas will now sing a Tudor song!

The maid was in the garden hanging out the clothes, when down came a blackbird and pecked off her nose!

Come, buy my fresh water!

Water'll kill ye!

Verily, mine's purer.

Buy our freshly brewed beer.

Oink, I love a good dung heap!

And one for baby.

THERE WAS NO RUNNING WATER AND LITTLE WAS UNDERSTOOD ABOUT HYGIENE OR GERMS ·

The Spare Prince

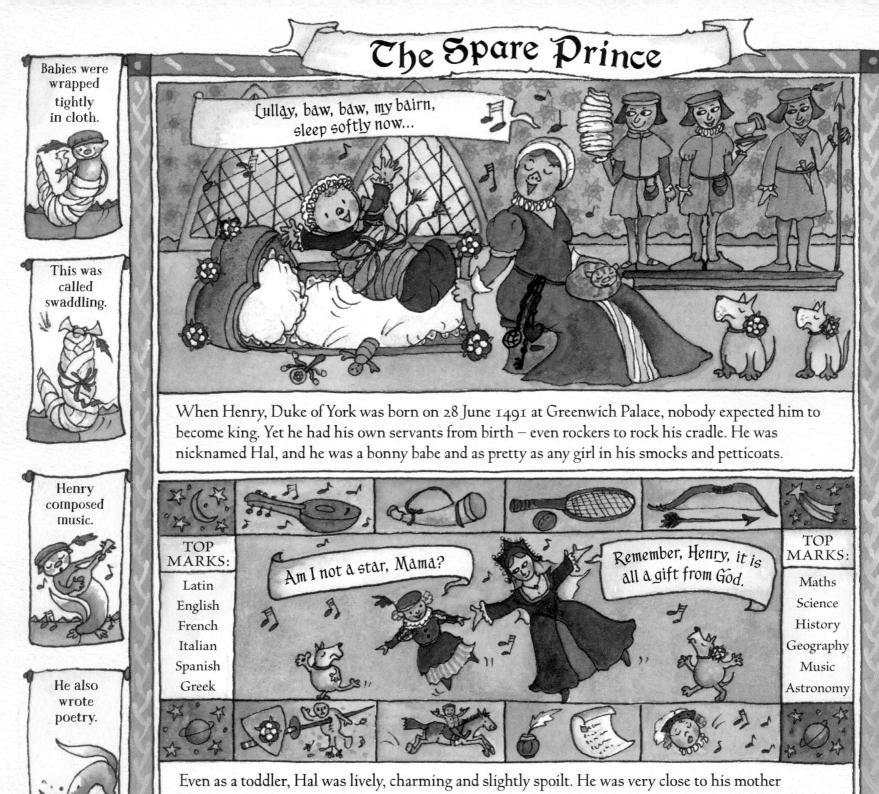

When Henry, Duke of York was born on 28 June 1491 at Greenwich Palace, nobody expected him to become king. Yet he had his own servants from birth – even rockers to rock his cradle. He was nicknamed Hal, and he was a bonny babe and as pretty as any girl in his smocks and petticoats.

TOP MARKS:

Latin
English
French
Italian
Spanish
Greek

TOP MARKS:

Maths
Science
History
Geography
Music
Astronomy

Even as a toddler, Hal was lively, charming and slightly spoilt. He was very close to his mother Elizabeth. She encouraged him in everything he did and he pleased her by excelling at all his lessons. He was also fantastic at sports, including tennis, archery, dancing, hunting, riding and jousting.

A line from Prince Hal's pen: "The time of youth is to be spent, But vice in it should be forfent." (Forfent means forbidde

• MEDICINES WERE MOSTLY MADE OF HERBS AND INSECTS • COMMONERS COULDN'T

Now you're my heir, you must sleep in my bed chamber.

Father, do not ask this of me!

Hark, I growl.

Hal was only eleven when his brother Arthur died and he became heir to the throne. It was a bit of a shock! Suddenly, he was expected to give up dangerous sports and spend more time at court.

One brother is as good as another.

Shall we dance the volta?

My lord!

Hal's father told him to get engaged to Arthur's widow, Catherine of Aragon. She was seventeen – six years older than Hal. Yet she was bright, funny and enjoyed sports. Better still, she had a pet monkey and loved to dance, so the betrothed couple got on very merrily.

The king was always well guarded at night.

A dog or ferret on your bed protects you from fleas!

Young Hal always said his prayers...

They say hell's flames will get you if you don't!

We never bite priests. We don't want to go to hell!

My body aches.

Skin of a donkey!

Doesn't the donkey need it?

My head aches.

Hangman's rope!

I've got the plague.

You're on your own, mate!

AFFORD DOCTORS · DOCTORS USUALLY HAD NO IDEA WHAT CAUSED DISEASE! ·

Henry VIII ~ The Headstrong

Hal was a spark of life after his dad.

Hal loved his new wife to bits!

She was so charming and kind ...

she could almost have been a ferret!

Spanish blood is very tasty!

We'll call him Bluff King Hal.

He's right royal.

Verily, he's 6' 4" tall.

A king<u>ly</u> stature.

In April 1509, just before Hal's eighteenth birthday, his father Henry VII died. Hal and Catherine were married shortly afterwards. Then on 24 June, with great pomp and ceremony, Hal was crowned King Henry VIII and Catherine was crowned as his queen. Their coronation was a day of joy, for this handsome young prince brought new hope to his kingdom. Two days of jousting and feasting followed.

'Tis an auspicious day!

You're right, there.

There's fairy magic about.

Aye, bread magically vanishes!

That's not magic, that's thieving!

· A CORONATION WAS A CHANCE FOR COMMONERS TO CELEBRATE ·

HENRY AND CATHERINE'S CORONATION TOOK PLACE ON MIDSUMMER'S DAY

Pongs and Palaces

Hal loved clothes and jewels.

Hal loved mattresses too.

Lots of them!

It took ten men to make his bed and search it for assassins.

It took millions of fleas to fill it!

Not bad for a butcher's son!

Wolsey, who had started life as a butcher's son, loved fine palaces and buying expensive things.

Thy ring is beauteous!

I thought so, too.

Unfortunately for Wolsey, Hal also loved expensive things and fine palaces.

Just one more castle... Yes, my lord!

Hal had inherited seven palaces and fourteen castles, but enough was never enough for Hal.

No rush, but move out by tomorrow!

When Wolsey rebuilt Hampton Court Palace, Hal liked it so much he pinched it!

My ladies are not yet packed.

Then they are behind the hour!

When Hal got bored, or a palace began to smell, he would just move to another one. His courtiers, his many hundreds of servants and all his furniture travelled with him.

We got the handsomest king in Europe.

He's a true royal!

But does he care about us poor folk?

Poverty is God's punishment for our sins. Or for Hal's sins...

· COMMON FOLK LOVED HENRY EVEN THOUGH THEIR LIVES DID NOT GET ANY EASIER ·

Rats!

Even the rats avoid Lord Stinkard!

Cast thine eyes down!

'Tis a fine and kingly easement.

As there were no drains and waste wasn't cleared very often, palaces quickly became smelly. At Hampton Court there was a room of lavatories called the Great House of Easement which could sit 28 courtiers at a time – what a pong! Hal had his own velvet-covered lavatory and a Groom of the Stool to wipe his bum. He often suffered from constipation – methinks he ate too much meat. In one year his court ate 8,200 sheep, 2,330 deer, 1,870 pigs, 1,240 oxen, 760 calves, 53 wild boar and zero ferrets!

Hal had a huge appetite.

He often ate thirteen-course meals.

On feast days he ate swan and peacock.

He loved strawberries and milk jelly!

As Hal grew older his blood grew rancid!

Lose your head or go to hell.

That's the Tudor choice.

Oh, but we love our Hal.

That we do.

While he eats peacock, we eat turnips.

Baa!

· THE POPULATION BEGAN TO GROW AND MORE PEOPLE WERE OUT OF WORK ·

The Field of the Cloth of Gold

When Hal came to the throne, he wanted to prove what a fine warrior he was, so he stirred up old quarrels with France and Scotland. His general, the Earl of Surrey, defeated the Scots at Flodden Field, killing King James IV of Scotland. Meanwhile, Hal won a battle against the French. Then, in 1520, Francis I, the French king, invited Hal to Calais to talk peace and play games of skill. Francis wanted Hal to be his ally as he was surrounded by the realms of the Holy Roman Emperor, Charles V: Spain, Holland and Germany.

· MANY COMMONERS WERE RECRUITED INTO THE ARMY · THOUSANDS LOST

Both Hal and Francis were very fond of sport and display and were determined to outshine each other. There was such an array of jewels and finery that the gathering became known as "The Field of the Cloth of Gold". Hal was jealous of the French king's good looks and was most upset when Francis beat him at wrestling. He only recovered after he proved himself the better archer! The two monarchs failed to reach an alliance and Hal continued to pick quarrels with France for the rest of his reign.

"The Catholic Church does not allow divorce." I'm going to lose my head!

Wolsey tried very, very hard to persuade the Pope to permit Hal's divorce, but without success.

Prithee, prithee, prithee!

I am queen. This cannot change.

He then tried to get Queen Catherine to retire to a nunnery, but she refused.

All you have done is worth nothing if you can't do this!

Hal was furious. He would have beheaded Wolsey if the poor man hadn't fallen ill and died.

I'll set up my own church!

Hal decided to break with the Catholic Church and become head of the Church of England.

I grant myself a divorce. Now I can marry Anne.

Once a queen, always a queen!

This meant Hal was more important than the Pope so he could give himself a divorce, which he did! Now he was free to marry his younger love, Anne Boleyn. She was sure to give him a son and heir!

Hal turned against Wolsey.

He took all Wolsey's money and palaces.

Hal declared his daughter, Mary, illegitimate.

He hardened his heart against her.

He flicked her away like a flea!

Was it poaching or treason, mate?

This'll cure your chilblains!

A witch or not a witch, that is the question!

PILLORY, THE STOCKS, TORTURE, HANGING, AND EVEN BURNING AT THE STAKE ·

CATHERINE of ARAGON

Thou hast grown old and wrinkled.

Thou hast grown old and crabby.

Hal was married to Catherine for 24, mostly happy, years. He jousted as "Sir Loyal Heart" and laid trophies at her feet. She bore Hal six children, but they all died except for Mary, born in 1516. Hal divorced Catherine when his wish for a son became overwhelming. After the divorce, she left court and never saw her daughter again. She died in 1536, still calling herself Queen Catherine.

ANNE BOLEYN

Thy neck is so tempting!

My neck is yet young, my king.

Hal's marriage to Anne in 1533 divided England. Many people stayed loyal to Catherine and the Church of Rome. Anne had a daughter, Elizabeth, in September 1533. Then she miscarried a baby boy. Hal was furious and wanted to divorce her. His minister, Thomas Cromwell, advised against a second divorce, so Anne was accused of courting other men. This was treason, so Anne was beheaded.

Henry began to behave most unkindly.

A ferret never casts off his wife!

Anne was clever and feisty.

A French swordsman beheaded her.

Divorced, beheaded ...

JANE SEYMOUR

My dearest and best wife.

Henry was 45 when he married Jane.

He was balding and growing portly!

Swans symbolize love and loyalty.

Jane was a lady-in-waiting to Anne. She refused Hal's advances while he was married, but in 1536, eleven days after Anne's execution, she married him. Jane blamed Anne for Hal's break with the Pope and his mistreatment of English Catholics. She wanted to influence him for the better. On 12 October 1537, their son Edward was born. After 28 years and three marriages, Hal had a male heir at last! Sadly, twelve days later, Jane died. Hal was heartbroken. He was buried beside Jane when he died.

... died.

In May 1539, Hal ordered Cromwell to find him another wife. Finally, Hal picked Anne of Cleves, the sister of a German duke. When Anne arrived in England she did not resemble the flattering portrait that Cromwell had shown Hal, but it was too late to stop the wedding. Hal couldn't upset the German duke by beheading Anne, so he divorced her and beheaded Cromwell!

Hal married Catherine in 1540, on the day Cromwell was beheaded. She was nineteen and Hal was 49. Thomas Cranmer, head of Hal's new Church, was not keen on Catherine as she was a Catholic. He told Henry she'd had boyfriends before him – which was true! This was treason, so Catherine was beheaded after only eighteen months of marriage. Her boyfriends were executed too.

KATHERINE
PARR

I have my fool to make me laugh and you to rub my toes.

Verily!

Henry's fool was named Will Somers.

Nobody else dared to tease Henry like Will did.

Henry believed worms could cure him.

There's no fool like an old fool.

When Hal and Katherine Parr got married in 1543, he was 52 and not a great catch! He was so fat he could hardly walk and had to be carried on a special chair. His lungs were bad, he was constipated, he had gout, leg ulcers, bouts of fever and was very grouchy. Katherine was a kind, obedient wife and a devout believer in the Church of England. She was loved by Hal's children, Mary, Elizabeth and Edward, and she brought them to live together at court for the first time. Katherine remained married to Hal until he died.

... survived!

The Death of Bluff King Hal

Hal signed execution warrants on his deathbed.

Hal's split with the Catholic Church led to a conflict...

Protestants fought Catholics.

Catholics fought Protestants!

Fleas fought for blood!

That's my boy.

In early January 1547, Hal felt too ill to spend time with his queen or even his beloved fool. He retired to bed, and on 28 January he died aged 55. Hal left England poorer and in a state of religious turmoil: the new Protestants who wanted worship to be simpler were fighting with the Catholics. Thousands of people had been executed during his reign and thousands of others had died in pointless wars. What had happened to Bluff King Hal whose coronation had brought hope and joy? Had he damaged his brain in a jousting accident? Or had he just become a cruel tyrant? It may never be known. Yet in his "great matter" Hal had succeeded – he had left a son, Edward, to carry on the Tudor dynasty!

Who will feed us now?

Hal did it for the best.

We'll starve.

I'll die.

The monks fed and clothed us.

They taught me Latin.

I had a job!

· HENRY CLOSED THE CATHOLIC MONASTERIES, SO THE POOR COULD NO LONGER TURN TO

The Short Reign of Edward VI

Hal's son was only nine when he became King Edward VI so his uncle, the Duke of Somerset, became Lord Protector and governed for him.

Edward and Somerset were both Protestants and upset the Catholics with new laws which banned many of their religious rites.

There was also growing discontent amongst the peasants as landowners stopped them renting plots or grazing their flocks on common land.

Somerset did little to restore harmony and in 1550 he was replaced by another Protestant, the Duke of Northumberland.

Three years later, Edward became ill and Northumberland began to worry about his safety if Mary, Edward's Catholic sister, became queen. He persuaded Edward to name Henry VIII's Protestant grand-niece, Lady Jane Grey, as his heir. In July 1553, Edward died and Northumberland declared Jane queen!

Queen Mary I

I've only got one religion.

FOOD!

I fight over it a lot.

But I always win!

You can guess our religion!

I have suffered enough humiliation in my life without that upstart!

QUEEN JANE 10-19 July 1553

I smell ferret!

Lady Jane Grey was fifteen when she was proclaimed queen. She had little claim to the throne and even Protestants believed Mary was the rightful queen. After only nine days, Queen Jane was overthrown and eventually both she and Northumberland were executed. Mary became queen, but her subjects were in for a shock! Mary had hated her father for heartlessly divorcing her mother and declaring her illegitimate. She had turned to her religion for comfort and now felt it her sacred duty to restore the Roman Catholic faith and purge England of Protestants.

KEEP OUT!

But they're my turnips.

Billy's hungry.

KEEP OFF!

But that's our grazing.

· WHEN LANDLORDS THREW COMMONERS OFF THEIR FIELDS AND ENCLOSED

Live here, good queen, live here, You are amongst your friends. Their comfort comes when you approach, And when you part it ends.

Majesty, I have built you your own tower, private garden, boating lake and hunting lodge.

Her skin is as white as a lily!

She looks like a goddess.

WARNING: the plague often hit London in the summer.

It was safer to leave the city when the weather was hot!

Moving about also helped avoid smelly loos.

Me and Arthur are keen on that!

Unlike her father, Bess had not inherited great wealth. She liked beautiful clothes and jewels, but sometimes she was forced to sell these to raise cash. In the summer, Bess saved money and met with her people by going on "progresses" around the country. Bess and her court would stay with nobles along the way. They were expected to entertain Her Majesty lavishly – even if it meant bankrupting themselves!

Rings on her fingers and bells on her toes, she shall have music wherever she goes."

'Ave you seen her?

She's pretty.

And clever.

And charming.

Long live Good Queen Bess.

· BUT ELIZABETH SOON WON HER SUBJECTS OVER WITH HER DEDICATION AND EASY CHARM ·

Mary, Queen of Scots

There were many plots against Queen Bess.

Many traitors were beheaded.

Mary wore a red petticoat for her execution.

Her dog hid underneath her petticoat.

There is a lot to be said for a good dog!

"You no good Catholic!" "You no good Protestant!"

Good Queen Bess had inherited a country split by religious discord.

"One's subjects must be moderate."

Bess was a Protestant, but although she was quick-tempered, she hated extremists.

"We will allow moderate Catholics."

She wanted both moderate Catholics and Protestants to be accepted and live in harmony.

"A Protestant can't be queen!"

Many people hated that idea. They wanted a Catholic monarch to rule the country.

"I am the most perfect of all Catholics."

Bess's cousin Mary, Queen of Scots, was a keen Catholic contender for the throne.

"Will you protect me, dear cousin?"

Mary fled to England after her husband died. Many people believed she'd had him murdered.

"Throw away the key!"

Bess knew Mary was after her crown so she locked her up for the next nineteen years.

"Shh! This letter will be the death of the queen!"

Unfortunately, this did not stop Mary plotting against our Good Queen Bess.

"Farewell, world!"

Finally, Bess lost patience with Mary. In 1587, she signed Mary's death warrant.

"We are charmed to meet you."

"Please, heal me."

"All them jewels! She's a picture."

"Heal my puppy."

The Spanish Armada

The death of Mary, Queen of Scots did not end the Catholic threat. King Philip II of Spain also wanted England to be a Catholic country again. In 1588 he invaded England with a fleet of ships called the Armada. Our sailors loaded empty ships with gunpowder, set them on fire and then drove them towards the Armada. The Spanish sailors tried to turn their huge ships around, but in their hurry they bumped into each other. Then a great storm came and most of the Spanish ships sank!

I kissed her hand once.

Liar!

She's an angel.

Our guardian angel.

I love her.

Hurrah for Good Queen Bess!

THEM AND TOUCH THE SICK, AS THEY BELIEVED SHE COULD HEAL THEM ·

Sir Francis Drake

The Spaniards called Drake El Draco – The Dragon.

He stole their gold to give Queen Bess.

Drake also lost our good queen's money.

Bess was most displeased and banished him from court!

Dragon's blood is too hot to swallow!

Gold for queen and country!

El Draco!

¡Vete al infierno!

Arise, Sir Francis.

I will arise and keep on rising!

Tarry a while, we have time to finish the Spanish and our game!

1540–1596

Both before and after the Armada, Spanish ships sailed to and from South and Central America and returned to Spain loaded with gold, silver and other treasure – a perfect target for pirates! Our dear queen, having no liking for the Spanish, turned a blind eye to English pirates who relieved them of their hoard. A favourite buccaneer was Sir Francis Drake. He was knighted by our gracious queen after becoming the first Englishman to sail around the world. Drake also helped lead the attack against the Spanish Armada, but they say he paused to finish his game of bowls first!

Come back soon!

What an adventure.

I can't swim.

· ELIZABETH ENCOURAGED FOREIGN TRADE, SO SEA PORTS FLOURISHED ·

Sir Walter Raleigh

It was tough being a sailor ...

eating nothing but salt meat, peas and bread ...

and trying to sail heavy ships.

Many sailors died at sea.

Wat and I eat Spaniards on potato for breakfast!

We do, Dad.

False love, desire, and beauty frail, adieu! Dead is the root whence all these fancies grew.

1552-1618

Majesty, you are my only Tudor Rose!

Verily, thou dost know how to treat a queen!

Majesty, I blush.

Creep!

Flea explorers travelled by rat!

Sir Walter Raleigh was another of Bess's favourite adventurers. Little mattered more to a Tudor noble than valour, gallantry and honour and Raleigh had ink pots full of these! He was a fearless soldier, a fine poet and was extremely handsome. He led many expeditions to America and introduced potatoes and tobacco to England. It is said he once threw his velvet cloak over a puddle so that Her Majesty would not dirty her dainty shoes. He did fall out of favour, though, when he secretly married one of Bess's ladies-in-waiting. He was locked up in the Tower of London until the queen forgave him!

No land, ahoy!

We'll starve.

I've lost all my teeth and hair!

Shall we mutiny?

Think of the rewards if we'd returned with treasure!

· THIS MEANT MORE JOBS BOTH ON LAND AND AT SEA, SO THERE WAS LESS POVERTY ·

Mr William Shakespeare

That very time I saw, but thou couldst not,
Flying between the cold moon and the earth,
Cupid all arm'd: a certain aim he took
At a fair vestal throned by the west,
And loos'd his love-shaft smartly from his bow
As it should pierce a hundred-thousand hearts;
But I might see young cupid's fiery shaft
Quench'd in the chaste beams of the watery moon,
And the imperial votaress passed on,
In maiden meditation fancy free.
~ A Midsummer Night's Dream, Act II, Scene 1

Bess banned religious plays to stop unrest.

Secular plays were much more fun!

I fancy I would make a marvellous actor!

Bravo, Will!

Eek!

Our Good Queen Bess encouraged not only trade and exploration but also the arts, which are far closer to the heart of a scribe. Bess's court was a haven for writers, poets, scholars, musicians and dramatists. Jubilations! Our dear Majesty was a generous patron, especially to one Mr William Shakespeare, an actor and playwright of great repute. I have even had the honour of transcribing one of his plays! Londoners still flock to the new theatres to watch them. Listen out for the theatre's trumpeter if you want to know when the play is about to start!

Theatres were alive with fleas!

'Ere, that toff called me a stinkard!

Well you are, mate.

Do you like Will or Mr Greene best?

Shut up and listen to the play!

I'd rather watch the bear-baiting!

Will is an upstart crow!

Eeeeeek!

· THE NOBILITY HAD SEATS IN THE NEW THEATRES, BUT THE STINKARDS,

'Ere, Will, you're meant to be speaking to me – Titania!

The king doth keep his revels here tonight.

The Globe Theatre opened in 1599.

Female parts were played by men or boys.

Some theatres were used for bear-baiting, too!

Many of Mr Shakespeare's plays were also performed at court, for as our dear queen grew older she was less inclined to venture into public places. I suspect that many of Mr Shakespeare's plays were written to keep his queen and patron sweet of temper and generous of mood. I myself was privileged to watch *A Midsummer Night's Dream*, which was written for a special court performance. Our Bess blushed with pleasure when the fairy king, Oberon, honoured her with some most flattering lines.

We used to perform in a flea circus.

Buy my fine apples!

Shh!

Shh!

Hot pies for sale!

I can't hear the words.

Ooh!

I know every line by heart ... ah, Juliet...

Ah, Romeo!

AS THE POORER COMMON FOLK WERE KNOWN, STOOD THROUGHOUT THE SHOW ·

Bess's dad would have been proud.

But Bess left no Tudor heir!

So it was out with the Tudors ...

and in with the Stuarts!

As Elizabeth had no children, she appointed a Protestant, James VI of Scotland from the House of Stuart, as the next monarch. The great Tudor dynasty had finally ended. There were over a thousand mourners in her funeral procession, including my good self, and thousands more lined the route. On top of the coffin lay an effigy of Queen Elizabeth dressed in her finest clothes. It was so lifelike that all who saw it gasped in wonder. Queen Elizabeth was buried in Westminster Abbey next to her half-sister, Mary, who had once imprisoned her in the Tower of London.

Henry would have turned in his grave!

Men can't rule!

My dad does!

It'll be that Scottish king, James VI.

He'll be James I of England.

A male monarch. It'll never work!

AND FEARED THAT A KING MIGHT NOT RULE AS WELL AS THEIR GOOD QUEEN BESS! •

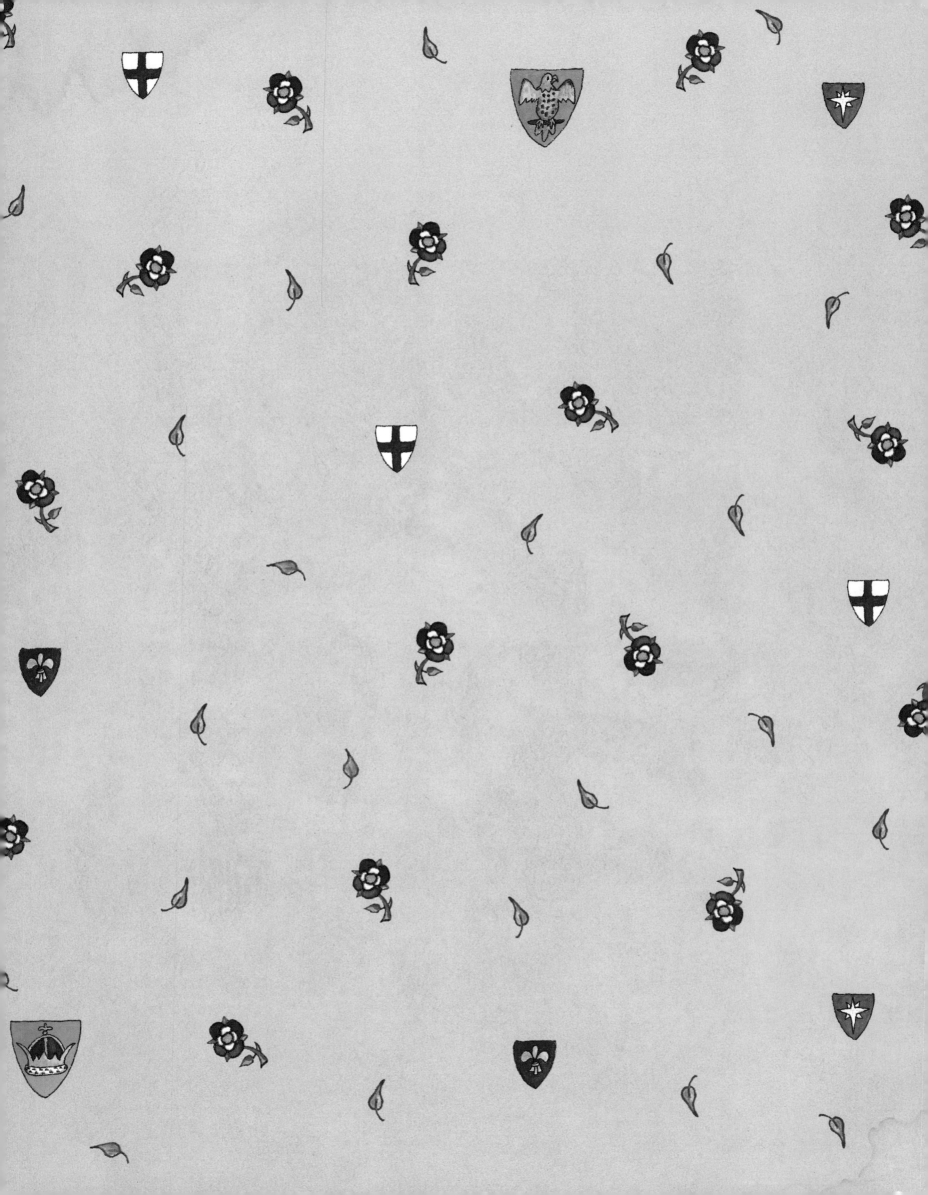

Marcia Williams

With her distinctive cartoon-strip style, lively text and brilliant wit, Marcia Williams brings to life some of the world's all-time favourite stories and some colourful historical characters. Her hilarious retellings and clever observations will have children laughing out loud and coming back for more!

ISBN 978-1-4063-5455-3

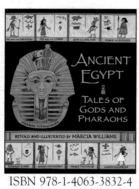

ISBN 978-1-4063-3832-4

ISBN 978-1-4063-5268-9

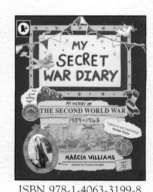

ISBN 978-1-4063-3199-8

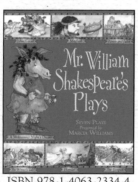

ISBN 978-1-4063-2334-4

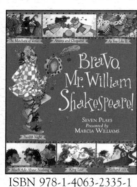

ISBN 978-1-4063-2335-1

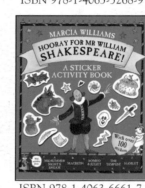

ISBN 978-1-4063-6661-7

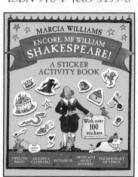

ISBN 978-1-4063-6660-0

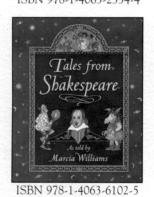

ISBN 978-1-4063-6102-5

ISBN 978-1-4063-4492-9

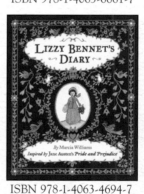

ISBN 978-1-4063-4694-7

ISBN 978-1-4063-6086-8

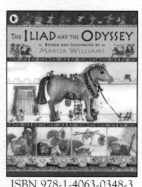

ISBN 978-1-4063-0348-3

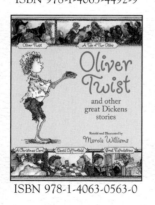

ISBN 978-1-4063-0563-0

ISBN 978-1-4063-0562-3

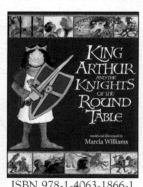

ISBN 978-1-4063-1866-1

Available from all good booksellers

www.walker.co.uk